# FROM VICTIM TO VICTORY

## *By the Mercy of God*

*Your past is not your identity Let go and obtain Freedom!*

Written By: Yamine Trotman

**FROM VICTIM TO VICTORY**

*Copyright © 2023 Yamine Trotman.*

*All rights reserved. No part of this book may be used or reproduced by any means, graphic, electronic, or mechanical, including photocopying, recording, taping or by any information storage retrieval system without the written permission of the author except in the case of brief quotations embodied in critical articles and reviews.*

*Because of the dynamic nature of the Internet, any web addresses or links contained in this book may have changed since publication and may no longer be valid. The views expressed in this work are solely those of the author and do not necessarily reflect the views of the publisher, and the publisher hereby disclaims any responsibility for them.*

*ISBN: 978-9-7682-9032-8 (sc)*

*Print information available on the last page.*

# *Contents*

Preface ..................................................................................ix

Introduction .........................................................................xiii

Chapter 1   My Childhood..................................................1

Chapter 2   High School .....................................................8

Chapter 3   A Loved one lost ............................................11

Chapter 4   A Turning Point of Love ................................16

Chapter 5   The Welcoming of a Gem ..............................20

Chapter 6   Did I miss the mark? .....................................29

Chapter 7   The lies I believed and letting go ...................34

Chapter 8   The End of it..................................................41

Chapter 9   Lesson well Learnt ........................................ 46

*From Victim to Victory*

*By the Mercy of God*

# *Dedicated To*

The Tabitha's Home for Women and Children. Tabitha's Home for Women and Children is a faith-based, non-profit organisation located in Mt. Pleasant, Tobago, which seeks to help women build/rebuild a constructive life for themselves and their children through the provision of a safe space where transformation can take place.

I also dedicate this to my kids for breaking generational curses; I know it has been trying.

Highest gratitude is given to Almighty God who allowed me the ability to move past my insecurities and who took me from **Victim to Grace** with a testimony.

In addition, I sincerely wish to thank my loving family; my husband Alfredo Martinez Cortes and children Abril and Giselle. I also wish to thank my brother Witson Trotman and my cousin Stephenson Trotman for their continued love and support.

# *Preface*

As I commenced penning this script, I thought of softening the word of God so that anyone who does not believe in Jesus Christ can benefit from it. However, after arriving at the third page I could not write anymore. The truth is everyone can benefit from the full record.

God has been instrumental in my life and in this book. All the experiences recorded in this book were only survived by me due to the Love and Grace that God has for me and has bestowed upon me.

I believe that Jesus came to this earth. He lived, died, and was raised from the dead to deliver me from my sinful nature and that He is the Son of Almighty God. I also believe that there is a Father, a Son, and a Holy Spirit and that whoever believes in Him; Jesus Christ would have life, find true love, and will experience real peace at all times.

I profoundly believe that anyone without a belief would experience a very hard life. And will encounter difficulties in anything they pursue. Am I here to force you into serving God? No, rather, to tell you how the God factor literally saved my life.

I needed GOD in all aspects to even begin to make sense of all that I have been through and to even live.

I have been through more than I wish I had. But if I had another chance, I would ask for the same life and the same experiences. I really like me now! To be honest, that declaration took years to even become one. I hated my life for years and my deliverance took place over time.

Don't get me wrong, I am aware of the darkness that exists in individuals at times as a result of dark times; trust me, I know it's not easy to expel. It's like forgiving someone for wrong, but not forgetting they have wronged you. So too, is the relationship between me and my past; I made peace with my past and my mistakes. I look back and see the reasons why God put me through this path, even after my past **caused me a lot of pain,** I chose to use it as a steppingstone to my victory and so can you.

I'm thankful for the lessons I've learnt. I know as babies we cannot choose, or ask for the path that we are given, but earlier when I said, *if I had another chance, I would ask for the same life and the same experiences*, it's based on the person I am now. I really do like **who I have become,** and better yet; I have all the experience I need to handle every situation differently. Some mistakes were harder to get over, but as I said before, if it was not for Jesus, I would have remained at that stage; where I treat every individual who has wronged me and others as my forever enemies. **I choose to get over it, and it works.** I am here to tell about how I learned to accomplish not dying in the process of living.

The book of Genesis says, that when Joseph was sold by his brothers to the Egyptians, he had **chosen** to be proactive and in return, he was able to save his people from hunger. I profoundly believe that by writing my story, I too can save lives.

Joseph's brothers threw him into a pit, and he ended up in the palace. So, I was in this dark pit and managed to get out and find the light in which I am standing today.

Genesis 45:4-7

New International Version

⁴ Then Joseph said to his brothers, "Come close to me." When they had done so, he said, "I am your brother Joseph, the one you sold into Egypt! ⁵ ***And now, do not be distressed and do not be angry with yourselves for selling me here, because it was to save lives that God sent me ahead of you.*** ⁶ For two years now there has been famine in the land, and for the next five years there will be no plowing and reaping. ⁷ **But God sent me ahead of you to preserve for you a remnant on earth and to save your lives by a great deliverance.**

In the chapters to come, I will speak about my experiences, and it may feel to you as if I am throwing my parents under the bus but believe me, I now know that each human does the best with what they got and I now understand that even at the best and healthiest, anyone's love cannot be compared with God's love for us.

As time passes, I realize more and more that people are not open about their experiences with their parents, somehow excluding them from the equation of whom they have become.

Today's culture has taught us to deal with anxiety, pain, depression, and shame within our closed doors, even if it means going to sleep and waking up with the intense feeling that we cannot go on. That you constantly wish there was a "get me out button" to push while hiding your insecurities. "Fake it till you make it" is what they say, right? I do not believe in that statement when it comes to living my life. The word says that Jesus died for me to have LIFE and to have it more ABUNDANTLY.

Let's talk about what is hurting us and heal; for the word also says to confess our faults to one another so that we can be set free. Let us give testimonies of how we regain control of our life by surrendering and dropping all pretenses.

**Life was intended to be FULL.**

**You can CHOOSE to Make It,**

**Even if it does not start that way.**

# *Introduction*

Hi, my name is Yamine and I'm a pretty strong girl, at least I consider myself to be, in light of all the hardships, hiccups, and moments of insecurities I've experienced. It might sound a bit contradictory, that my negative experiences, I can actually conclude, birthed strength in me, but it's true; they have.

I grew up in Venezuela, born and raised for part of my life and, I escaped it all the same. One might ask, 'What is there to escape?' This is my story.

Many of my Life experiences have taught me lessons that have carried me through other faithful experiences. Truth be told, many of them I wished I was never privy to, many I thought unfair, most I've questioned because I could not come to terms with the 'Why me?', you know; Why did He choose ME? I guess there would never be a good enough explanation for that, the answer just would not suffice. Bitterness, resentment, disorder, strongholds, generational curses, sexual immoralities, bondage, confusion, sadness, laughter, pretence, anxiety, anger; so much emotion and things that I was dealing with unknowingly; to name a few coupled in one individual is not good enough, let alone in a child under the age of ten. If I'm being honest, and I am, the negative emotions far outweighed the positive ones.

In this book, I will present to you a reality often hidden, covered up, and even untold. The real struggle to stay alive in a dying world. However, at the same time, I will share how the emotional, physical, and social damage can be repaired, and you can be your best self. The only catch is, 'over time'. ***There is still hope!*** There is a God who is concerned with your situation and who will help you through it.

It took me years before I was able to see positivity in my hardships, but now I do and so can you. Don't give up on yourself. Don't you dare harbour negativity, sorrow, and unforgiveness!

In reality, pain and hurt can force you to give off negative behaviour, sometimes you can build a wall to protect yourself and repel every unwanted thing from your life, and this is what I did (Flight or Fight or Freeze behaviours). My wall stood up for years and years. Only to realise that while this wall avoided future hurt and disappointment, it was only to an extent. In fact, all the wall did was keep me hidden; my future was not spared. You see, what's already behind the wall are like seeds that keep growing every time the unwanted darts kept approaching the wall, and what you are open to on the other side are voices of condemnation for your unwelcoming behaviour. This causes the wall to give off both negative and positive benefits. My wall created an even more damaged me. I had so much pain that was piled up caused by the abandonment of people purposely or not who were supposed to care for me.

I can laugh at it now; looking back at the purpose of this Yamine I had created to protect me.

The experiences of my life have caused me to feed off my anger, pains, and resentment for years. It was only when I was able to face it, that I was able to fix it. I first had to acknowledge that the issues existed, take them to GOD, and allow Him to lead me into dealing with them all, and today I do not regret it.

The truth is; there was no magic wand that was waved and it all passed away nor was there a quick fixing of relationships that took place, rather, it IS STILL A WORK IN PROGRESS; I AM. I deal with it daily and I pray often for God's guidance.

*How we react to the events that happen to us affect our daily life. And so, it dictates our future. Our destiny is formed by the decision we make about how we feel about our mistakes.*

# 1

# MY CHILDHOOD

Morning usually symbolises a fresh start, a time away from the past, and that meant whatever came with it. Morning should be a breath of fresh air, or how about a new life, literally speaking. Not for me, though. For me it was a different day with the same adventure. Little did I know, my "morning" was actually in the making and would show itself several years later.

My morning routine usually involved a rush to the kitchen to begin my morning devotion with my friend on the radio. Every morning like clockwork I would bask in the music that it offered to my ear. I would dance and sing loudly while gazing to the picture on the kitchen wall which portrayed an image of deity. I often conversed with the image and in my innocence with this combination, unknowingly lift my hands and offered worship to the picture I thought was God.

I was usually the first to rise on mornings, after my mother that is. My mother usually left at six a.m. for work. My family at this time consisted of mom, dad and my three siblings; two brothers and one sister. Mom was usually out to work in the early hours of the morning, so I never saw her much. As scarce as she was in the morning, so is my memory of her. I do remember, however, the times she would comb my hair, and this is due to the pain I experienced when she did. She usually pulled it. My mother worked continuously; one might say she was quite hard-working. However, it allowed her to be absent in my eyes, an absence which did more bad than good.

Prior to leaving for work on mornings, most times she left a tray of arepas for us in the refrigerator and we usually cooked it on the baking stone and had it for breakfast. Or, she might bake bread and pack our lunch kits for school; she baked a lot.

I sometimes thought ill of her and grew resentment towards her for years.

But a while after, a very long while after that is, I began looking at my mother from a different perspective and saw something different. Not dismissing the issue of her absence, though. I instead concluded the issue with the explanation of my mother's own childhood and what she experienced, and therefore, I eventually believed that my mom's actions were actually genuinely what she knew to do. I even saw her constant baking as her distress technique.

For the most part, I think I used to avoid my mother, or she used to avoid me. The bottom line is, as kids, we were mostly alone.

My siblings and I had experienced joyous times in our childhood. There were times we were allowed to play with the neighbours and the fun of our primary school days brought added excitement. One of my memorable experiences is that of running away from school or skipping school; I usually did every Thursday. It was a usual practice for my school to end half days not for dismissal but for extra-curricular activities on Thursdays. However, my extra-curricular activities involved me ditching school and remaining unseen while doing so. When I skipped school, I usually wore a black t-shirt below my school shirt and removed it to avoid being seen. Truth be told, I was actually getting away with it. After a series of successful getaways, and plans on stream for the next as usual; 'it rained on my parade'; I got caught.

I snuck away from school through the yard during the break period; made a clean get away and went to the mall. While there I spotted a teacher in the distance, my job now became playing hide and seek, such a fun turn of events. But Miss Sandy spotted me from a far distance and called out to me, "Janine," (my home name) "why aren't you in school!" Imagine the shock and embarrassment at the mall. Miss Sandy even threatened to call my father, which she did. Daddy came to the school, but I was not scolded, he just gave me a warning to not repeat such actions; I guess it was the least he could do. After all, your parents are supposed to nurture and protect you, and these are just two of the things I would gladly welcome. I wonder why a kid my age would be skipping school. It would have been nice if he asked me.

I attended a school, located opposite a Roman Catholic Church, so Roman Catholic became my religion; this was all I knew on the spiritual side of things. I was active in the school choir and our school choir sang in the church. I was also very active in the clubs at school as well and teachers were my friends; they looked out for me, and I was always willing to assist.

Primary school was enjoyable. I was also a fighter in school, but on the contrary, I was always defending someone. I was an advocate for my friends. I was also given a book to sign for my fighting accounts. In all this, however, I was an intelligent student.

I was unique in school with my dress code, even with my uniform, and I wore my socks up to my knees. Another one of my happy moments was swinging on the swings at the playground. I just loved the thrill of it; a trait I still hold dear to even now.

When we came home from school, mom usually left food for us in the refrigerator. Dad was not usually at home; he was at his regular drinking spot. We were not sad about him not being at home, though. His absence allowed us to watch different shows on the television; freedom, one might say.

Before heading off to school, we also had the task of taking our little brother to the babysitter, locking the house upon leaving. My babysitting adventure was not always an easy one. One day, my siblings and I took him to the sitter and left for school, however, he did not want to be there. When we got home from school that evening, we found him seated alone by the roadside. My brother sat there from seven in the morning until two in the afternoon and he was just three years old. He was headstrong on being stubborn towards going to the sitter, and from that day onwards he bravely stayed home alone. Mom and dad were not aware of his behaviour at first, however, when mom did learn of this, she left him at home and left food available for him, this continued until his pre-school started.

**Parenting is so unpredictable, even for the kids.**

Due to our upbringing, we all grew with a sense of independence. The constant neglect trained us to be self-sufficient. I was six at the time, my elder brother was seven, and my sister was the eldest. Though my siblings and I had a small age difference, communication in our family was not a common thing. I often found solace in my brother. My elder sister was wicked to me and so our relationship was not open and welcoming. The neglect of my mother stunted my relationship with her and, well, my father's lifestyle created a void that echoed throughout the household.

My father was a fighter; he was compassionate but rather physical. His comfort was alcohol and his addiction emanated acts of injustice. My father fought with my mother on a weekly basis. Things were thrown across the house in anger, and the verbal expressions were abusive and destructive they were like daggers to the heart.

Dad also carried a permanent frown which he gained from frowning a lot. I remember I used to sit on his lap and constantly try to smooth out his frown lines.

Daddy was happy when he was intoxicated; this is when we were allowed to go outside to play. On the other hand, his drunken state contributed to the abuse in the home. Mom and dad had problems communicating with each other as well. Their conversations always ended up in violent conflict.

Daddy was not as absent as mummy was, but it was not all a bed of roses. I didn't have much love for my father because of his reoccurring actions. Daddy was abusive, physically, mentally, emotionally, and sexually. The worst for me being sexually, my sister and I were both sexually abused by my father. It occurred like a dream, at nights when we were asleep. At first, I thought it was a dream, however, when I shared the ordeal with my sister it was as though we both had the same dream, which to me was no coincidence; it was actually happening. Years later, when we mentioned this to our mother her response was, why did we not tell her, otherwise she would have gotten him imprisoned. Like I said, any explanation for my mishaps will not be the right one. The experience of being sexually molested by my father was just another threader on the stairs of my dysfunctional, damaged life and I was not about to deal with my mother's unnecessary words at this late hour. And so, I blocked out discussing this issue as it silently affected me mentally, physically, emotionally, and socially and was shown in my everyday life.

My childhood forced me into maturity through responsibility, involuntarily. So, my transition into teenage years flowed smoothly with many, many, many, many bumps, potholes, skid marks, whatever you want to call it in the road.

*I was left with so many questions on parenting. I wondered if parents are consciously aware (when they are hurting their children), of their actions. You know the phrase, 'hurting people, hurt people', it is no respecter of persons. My parents were victims of bad parenting. But, the thing is, it's not the responsibility of the child or children to know this, nor to fix their past. It is, therefore, that of the parents.*

*I, however, respect my parents and forgive them for all their treatment, because by doing this I broke the pattern that was being passed on from my grandmother to my mother then to me.*

*If you do not forgive your parents, you will be an enhance version of your parents. But you will carry on with the learned behaviour.*

# 2

# HIGH SCHOOL

On exiting the primary school level of schooling, I entered highschool with great anticipation. I was a bright young girl, and I had a small group of friends, but I always had a relationship with my teachers, so they kept a close eye on me. If they saw the company I kept would lead me down a wrong path, I was warned of it; they were my parents at the school.

I was popular, yet on the inside of me I was not; I was lonely and in need of a rescue. You see, the person my peers were so eager to befriend was the character which stood in the place of my hurt, pain, anger, resentment, and my insecurities. No, it wasn't the real me, and I mostly believe my peers knew it. I answered yes to every request because I didn't want anyone to turn away from me, I couldn't handle another rejection, and so, I hid the real me. Did I get used? Yes, I did. Was I misused? Yes, I was, but those feelings were not as severe as the past and the then-hidden present.

I seldom stayed at home during these years, I got a job and sometimes I stayed by friends, home was everywhere for me. I was studying hard and excelling at my academics while working. However, the approval I sought, and sadly I can say to this day I still do, was that of my mother.

Mother wasn't active in my high school days as I would have liked her to be. Our relationship never improved. We were on an acquaintance level and that was not the best, nor was it healthy. I was difficult to deal with at a time; because I held so much negativity on the inside. I began doing things that were not right, also skipping school again to go where I should not. I was warned for having the wrong friends, but did not take heed.

Truth be told, my main reason for my delinquent behaviour was to get back at my mother, I felt she wronged me, I was the victim and I needed to administer revenge. As a result, however, I wasted a number of years, sacrificed a lot of joy, and sacrificed myself in the process with no betterment to my situation.

Where was my father in all this? Well, dad never returned home. Call me cruel, but I really didn't miss my dad, we were somewhat happy that he left. When dad left, the house was different, the quarrelling and fighting had ceased. What I missed, however, was a father, not my father.

At last, it was time for me to graduate. My graduation was wonderful. I was greatly assisted by my friends for my graduation. This was the time my mother got an opportunity to travel and she took it. She never attended my graduation. Just as she was absent throughout my high school years, so it was for my grand day. Nevertheless, I loved my mother; I just wish things were better.

*Note to parents,*

*Parents, you see those simple words, 'I love you'? Please say it to your kids, they need to hear it. And don't stop there; support it with your actions. And that if you do not repair the past it will continue to spoil your future relationship with your children.*

You know, as I grew older and got in touch with God, I came to the realisation that the past, if not dealt with, will show up in your future, whether you invite it or not.

# 3

# A LOVED ONE LOST

After dad left, my brother had a difficult time dealing with the loss. He became angry and emanated it in his actions. He exhibited acts of violence in his behaviour as well, as though blame was attributed to someone for dad leaving.

Dad left when we were still very young and mom left in our later years. Nevertheless, we still had to deal with both.

When dad left, a big part of my brother went with him. He and father had a special relationship. They went out a lot and dad liked going out with him. He was quiet and reserved; well behaved and he did not ask dad for anything on their trips, unlike me. Dad often expressed a great enjoyment in spending time with him.

My brother was eleven years old when dad left; one year older than I. A few months after dad's leaving he started asking for him.

At the time of dad's leaving, we lived in a rental apartment. Dad had paid months' worth of rent in advance to sustain us. However, there came a time when paying rent was not as easy as dad leaving money. We encountered this issue and our landlord's family wanted us evicted. So, thinking about dad leaving was just one of our problems, not the priority.

Stress showed up in our family and also in my brother and this he directed to mom. My brother's relationship with our mother was similar to mine with her; distant, and well, far away.

I must say though, dad leaving us, though the fighting with mom, drinking, and other negatives were gone, left a huge communication void in our home; no family conversations took place and we were already limited in communication. We just never spoke about it. Instead, we all bottled our feelings and kept them as our souvenirs, when we should have let them free. Anger, pain, hurt, discouragement, and frustration to name a few, now existed in all of us, growing and bearing fruits.

*A word of advice dear readers…*
*Be with the right crowd and watch your thoughts*

We eventually moved from our apartment and built a house on a piece of land. We built the house as a family out of galvanize. The physical house being built as a family was to be a symbol of us rebuilding our 'home'; our family unit that has been broken, battered, and bruised. Joy, peace, and laughter were our urgent necessities. Our home rebuilding project was doing well, we were developing a sense of stability and it was evident.

Sadly, within a year's time, things took a left turn. Mother was stressed out, my sister had problems of her own and my brother blamed our mother for dad leaving. Our 'home' was dysfunctional once more.

*How can a dysfunctional home become functional? Is there a handbook to fix it? Who has to fix it? What should be done? were* questions to which we needed answers.

My brother got involved with the wrong crowd and stopped attending school. He was also introduced to drugs which proved more and more detrimental as the days passed.

As much as my brother missed my dad, he inherited some of his traits. He abused mom in many ways; he sometimes 'beat' her, he cursed her, he would pelt her with stones and kept attacking her. Basically, he blamed mom for dad leaving us.

By this time, I was 12 years old and at home. The only thing was, home was not much of a happy place. I grew tired and frustrated with the dysfunction in my home and as a result, at age 12, I left home. Where would a twelve-year-old go, you may ask? I was well taken care of; I was going to school and was very successful at that, and in the evenings I was working. This I successfully did for years.

Close to my completion of primary school, I received a call from my sister with a plea from my mom to control the household. My mother was requesting that I return home. She also contacted me herself confirming what my sister had said. She declared that I was like a glue to hold the family together. She also said my brother only listens to me, no one listens to anyone and they needed me. I paid heed to mom's request and returned home. My family's state was just as mom had said.

My brother was still angered and needed help. I was thirteen years old when I returned home and I took on more responsibility by becoming a young entrepreneur. I started working in the dirt-digging industry. I was even digging dirt for septic tanks and it did great financially. This became a business for me, I began taking on jobs and hiring others to work and I was also able to successfully pay them. I also sold sand and made money; this is how I was able to fulfil my ice cream and snacks desire, after all, I was still a kid.

Mom was still working, but she started drinking, smoking, and liming again. Working made me lose interest in school, but my mother was not about to have me drop out of school, and so she persuaded me to go back to school for which I am grateful. I was doing very well at school and was soon to graduate. I obeyed my mother and went back to school and was also the only one of my siblings to graduate.

I continued on to high school, however, I was in and out of home. I later graduated from high school and moved on with my life and eventually had a daughter. I continued working, while living at home with my siblings; two brothers and one sister, mom had left us and went to another country.

My brother still carried on in an angry manner. One day when I came home from work, he was rocking the house with music. Mom was not around; she had already left. We were a sibling household family type. I worked and brought in groceries and I also had my daughter.

So on this account I came home from work and Calvin was rocking the house with music, I walked over to the stereo and turned the music down. My brother was so enraged that he broke all the windows in the house. I was honestly fearful for my daughter's life.

I asked Calvin if he wanted help with his problem and he did want help. I, however, became fearful for my daughter's life, so I left with my daughter. My brother was left with my sister and other brother at home and I guess the pain of neglect caused him to commit suicide.

*A family is a unit; all members whoever they are contribute to its singleness. When one member is missing, a void appears on the inside of the others.*

*Word of advice: the bible states in the book of Romans 12: 10 KJV*

*Be kindly affectioned one to another with brotherly love; in honour preferring one another;*

*Look out for each other. Do not take each other for granted.*

# 4

# A TURNING POINT OF LOVE

At age eighteen I met a guy who changed my view on life. With him, I actually believed my life was not meant to be all it had seemed to be. A light in the dark tunnel, not just the usual end of the tunnel as I have often sought before, but a beam of light so bright, it shone on me and made me feel warm and all jolly inside. My love was the epitome of care and change. What do I know, I was only eighteen, a very experienced eighteen wanting change. So ask me, was he my soulmate? Was he the right person for me? Was it to be as it was? Well, just as my answer is for my life, *I'd say, I don't know; as it is, the powers that be aligned it to be so.* But I am grateful, eternally.

One day on my shift at the supermarket where I worked my second job as a cashier, I came across this gentleman and he made my acquaintance. He was thirty – two, I was eighteen. Personally, I wondered where my mom was that she allowed me to even go out with him. Andrew was my first boyfriend; he was an experienced man and I was innocent on the issue. However, I learned.

Andrew was a smooth, sweet talker, a man in the service, highly respected by his peers and others around him. He was abusive, but not to me. He was a jealous man; possessive and controlling but no one had ever loved me like he did before.

I was blinded by love; blinded by his love and I did not mind it at all. You see, overall, Andrew was a nice man, I considered him my escape from my past. He loved me and paid attention to me, and with him I built my self-esteem. The pit that sunk me once previously, was now freely letting me out like it had no choice, no longer could I fit in that pit.

Andrew never took advantage of me I thought, even though he was knowledgeable of my situation, on the contrary, he always sought to build me. I was always encouraged to build my life. My love made me take a computer course and gave me my first cell-phone, in a way being with him made me change my way of thinking. Was I naive to have trusted him and put him so high in my life? Truth is, I adored Andrew.

Andrew took me everywhere and our relationship was an exciting one…

One day, Andrew and I had a date, I was supposed to meet him at the square, which I did. I sat there waiting patiently but, unusually, Andrew was late, the thing is he was always on time; his punctuality was a plus, another quality I adored about him. However, today he was not, I sat waiting on him for hours.

After a few hours, I went home and Andrew was there, he thought he had told me to meet him at home. I was really upset. Andrew, however, insisted that we go out; he still wanted to take me with him. We made a short journey out, Andrew brought me to my home and made his way to his. I was sure to inform him to call me when he arrived home. Sadly, Andrew never did.

That night I had a dream that all my teeth were crushed at the front of my mouth and exploding, and I spat them out one by one. I awoke out of sleep by the sound of someone calling me, however, no one was. Maybe it was symbolic of something significant as many dreams are, but I did not think much of it.

I went to work the next morning, still had not heard from Andrew, and someone told me, "Do you know that your boyfriend died last night?" I asked *which one*, and with a laugh I continued walking by. However, the word came to me was, "Do you know your boyfriend died last night?"

YES! It was my Andrew. This news hit me like a dagger piercing through my hope. I cried endlessly.

Andrew had acquired a motorcycle, which I personally never liked; he said he would, however, fix it and sell it, which he did but he same day he got the motorcycle back from the mechanic shop, the same day he died with it; my dreams was actually symbolic of me losing my Andrew, not just my Andrew, but a great symbol of hope in my life.

Andrew had children and this I was fully aware of and it was not an issue; we had plans to live together. At the funeral, there were also other women there, I held my end but conversed with his sister. I gave her items to put on his grave, which she did and she treated me as though I mattered. To add sugar to my coffee so to speak, my sorrow was momentarily quenched when she mentioned, that Andrew was going to take me to meet her and he felt he had really found a wife.

Andrew's passing was overwhelming for me. My relationship with Andrew lasted six months but I will not question the workings of the Almighty.

*This chapter was dedicated to Andrew*

# 5

# THE WELCOMING OF A GEM

The welcoming of a gem that is my daughter. *I love you, my love.*

When Andrew passed, I moved to Trinidad and stayed with my sister; born and raised in the country of Trinidad.

For me, however, it was a culture shock and a nerve-wracking experience. I was damaged; hurt and confused on entering a new environment and my sister was also. We were both two traumatized individuals in need of some serious healing.

Nevertheless, my visit to Trinidad improved my knowledge of my family; mom and other relatives. It's hard to learn that your already dysfunctional life was still missing more dysfunction. The sort of things you would see in a movie.

However, I left the island of Trinidad and moved back to Venezuela.

After coming back from Trinidad and Tobago I was a ticking bomb. I acquired work and residence at a hotel in Margarita island.

"In the eyes of the world this girl had no right to be pregnant." A year and a half later, in my own eyes, I thought the same thing.

I had just moved out from the hotel where I worked and lived because the manager sexually harassed me in the elevator. This thing kept happening to me. I could not understand what I used to do to deserve this behavior from men.

I made friends with a group of sexual workers that used to work in the corner of the hotel and they embraced me as a sister. I guess our stories were not so different. Hurting, lost people that found comfort in each other.

I moved to The Flamingo Hotel and I started working in the club as a dancer. There I met my gem's father. I think it was not an instant click because I avoided him for weeks. I was way too hurt to initiate any relationship. My mental state was fragile, and I was in a bad mood all the time. The only thing I remember was drinking, partying, and having random sex with strangers for money. I remembered my mother asking me what I was doing with my life, and I would think: *If she only knew that I was only physically alive.*

He showered me with money and gifts, but I was far from impressed. I was far too numbed.

One day he invited me to a party where I heard 'he throw the house out the window'; I say 'I heard' because I stood him up. I went to the cinema to watch a movie on my own. It was Scary movie 1. I never laughed so much in my life. It was funny out of this world. I remembered walking home and laughing out loud as if I was crazy.

I finally succumbed to his pleading. We started going out and I started spending time at his apartment; it felt like home. I had my own room and it was the most stability I had for the entire year.

I used to take care of him and his friends and in return, they used to pay my bills and keep me inside, safe.

After a few months, he started talking about a relationship and about how much he wanted a child with someone like me.

No one had ever asked me to build a future with them before. That blew my mind and I accepted at once. I used birth control for a while, eventually stopped and we started sexing with a purpose. Less than two weeks later I started to feel sick, and my body started changing.

I was pregnant! I did not know how to feel but to be honest, all the suicidal thoughts vanished, and I started to feel something that I never felt before. Hope. I felt hopeful, not like I did with Andrew, this was greatly different.

*I could not believe it. It was happening I finally will stop suffering and I will have a family of my own* I thought.

When I was three months into the pregnancy, this man came one day and changed into the devil himself. All the nice treatment ended with the words, "Honeymoon is over."

He started to curse me and treat me like the street worker he picked up. Telling all of his friends where he got me from. He forced me to put on his socks and to clean his feet. He also used to disappear for days and not tell me where he went. I just used to sleep and cry.

One day he was gone for three days and came back drunk and dirty. I could not believe he was the same sweet old man that made so many promises to me.

I made up my mind and packed my bags and asked him for passage to return home. I did it! He gave me exact change to reach home, not before telling me how unworthy I was of him, and even wishing me death. I silently just took every insult with the hope that he did not get physical. Honestly, I felt a release to know that it was finally over.

That experience was so traumatic for me that every time I heard a phone like his ring it used to give me strong anxiety attacks; this lasted for years.

Going home was good. My brother was still alive. Well obviously, I was judged. I left for good and came back pregnant with no father of the child. If that was my child, I will be overboard mad.

But as usual, my mom was who she was. Absent and lack of support. The only thing she said was I was crazy to leave the man. I could not believe my ears because I explained what had happened.

My belly grew and grew, and I became beautiful. And my mother behaved like my mother for the first time. She pampered me and taught me things about pregnancy and welcoming a baby.

During the pregnancy, I started to grow this fear inside of me that my child might be deformed and that someone could harm me and kill my child. Therefore, I started to be softer and more loving to others. Before this, I was so bitter that I used to ill treat everyone around me. So much so, that my neighbor wished me I made a dog.

I am thankful to God that I did not make a dog. But I made a beautiful baby. I remember someone telling me "You had to do something really good in this life to have made such a beautiful baby."

I woke up at 3:00 am that Wednesday morning. I had cramps like pain but I was excited, *finally,* I said. I sat in the living room in darkness holding my tummy, talking to my baby and thinking to myself, *was I was going to be able to be a good mom.*

My mom woke up as usual 5:00 am to get ready to go to work, "You scared me!" she said. She jumped when she had a glimpse of me in the dark living room. I told mom how I was feeling, and she told me that I was over-excited because my 'best friend' at the time and several other women were pregnant. However, I was the last and she told me I just wanted to make my baby.

I took a shower and went to the health center with my brother. When I arrived, they told me I had two dilations. Therefore, they referred me to the general hospital because of my anemic history, if I bleed out, they could not help me there.

I went and sat at my mother's job to wait for my brother to go home and bring my bags, as I did not walk with them because my mother did not believe I would be going into labor that day.

As I sat there no one believed I was in pain. After all, I had been feeling so much pain; I could take a punch and make it look like it did not hurt.

My brother took about an hour and a half to reach. When he finally showed up my mom paid a taxi to take us to the hospital. When we were almost there, I felt like a balloon burst, I even heard the noise and I said my water bag burst. But no fluid came out of me because I was sitting. As we pulled in front of the ER maternity, I stepped out of the vehicle and the amniotic fluid started running down my legs.

My brother was not allowed inside. There was a chaperon who will run up and down with news of the laboring moms on the second floor.

They took me to a cubicle where a doctor eating an empanada asked me if I was a Trinidadian. I guess he was just making conversation to keep me calm, but I was already calmed. He went on to say that he has been to Trinidad and that he loves it. I told him I was there once, and I was planning to return.

After the doctor was finished eating his meal, I asked him how he could eat and then just casually push his finger inside of us, he said he was used to it. *Obviously, he wears gloves I thought.*

He then proceeded with my checkup and found that I had five dilations and sent me inside. Another doctor came seeking my interest and he said, "She is ready."

He also asked, "Why aren't you screaming? I calmly answered, *the pain was not enough for me to scream.*

All the emotional pain I have been through prepared me; to this day, I can still bear pain in silence.

I was placed in the room with several women. Screams and curses echoed all around me. I lay quietly not knowing how to feel or what to say. So, I said or felt nothing until it was time.

**In life we may not be able to stop the pain from occurring but I think we can control how we deal with it.**

A nurse walked over to me together with my godmother's cousin who was in charge of the department. She explained what was about to happen and advised me to keep my mouth shut because air pulls the baby back up. I followed her advice and I was expecting to feel worse pain when I suddenly felt like I took the biggest dump of my life. I immediately called the nurse as they walked away and told her that my baby was here.

She asked me, "Have you made a baby before," and I answered no. She then questioned, "Well how you know;" I said *look*! She lifted the sweater I had on protecting me from the cold and she shouted BABYYYYYYYYYYYYYYYY! I never saw people run so fast. They were shouting, "Don't push, bring a wheelchair, don't close your legs, don't push." Their haste made me so nervous because I felt like I could kill my baby.

They placed me on the wheelchair and took me behind some curtains, opened my legs on a gynecological chair and told me not to push. I was opening my mouth so that the baby could go back up. Then I got the ok to push. My child just came out of me as if she was slipping on a playground slide.

My gem was a sight to behold; she was beautiful, white complexion, and her hair was so black and long. I had never seen anything more beautiful. In that moment, all my fears vanished, and I started to feel this love flowing in every part of me.

I understood at that point why God allowed me to make this child. I felt love for the very first time of my life. Seeing her watching me and holding on to me, caressing her warm skin, only GOD could have prepared me for this moment. Her smile was unique; she was born with a smile and laughing too. Yes, she used to just burst out a laugh without being prompted. I have never seen a newborn laugh like that. She laughed so much that she used to choke; that was scary though.

My child gave me the willingness to hope for a brighter future. Her birth is what has me here today. It constantly told me: **life is worth living**.

I can tell you today that this verse is true:

**Romans 8:28** KJV. *All things work together for good to them that love God, to them who are the called according to his purpose.*

# 6

# DID I MISS THE MARK?

Looking back, I remember for my eldest daughter's life I was so cold and distant. In other words, I became my mom.

I remembered swearing to myself that I will never become her, that I will not make the same mistakes. If or when I got the opportunity, I will not make the same mistakes. However, that turned out to be untrue, because we are what we do not heal from.

I did not know that then, but now I know. My mom taught me to be the only type of mother I knew to be. And we are who we learned to be because of our environment, experience, and interactions.

When my eldest daughter was growing, I was in survival mode all the time. I used to be exhausted and I had to drink every day to regulate my emotions.

I was a people pleaser, still being used. Being a people pleaser welcomes many insecure people that would use you for their gain. When you put a stop to them, they will be upset because you are no longer available. I lost a lot of friendships like that in my life.

I was not able to have a healthy relationship with anyone and that included my children. I used to yell at my kids, place blame on my kids, and overload my kids with adult stuff. Because my daughter was mature for her age as I was, I trusted her with way too much. Truth is, that was how I knew to raise them.

After gaining the strength to leave my second daughter's father, I used them as messengers because it was terrible to try to communicate with him. I was so emotionally immature that I did not know how to override his emotional abuse. So, we used to communicate the only way we knew, cursing and shouting.

The children were always the spectators. And because of my traumas and behavioral issues, I was always trying to win the argument. That used to make me look like the bad guy. I struggled with trying to control the situation, which I now know was unmanageable. I was in constant fight-or-flight mode.

Turns out the dysfunction I grew up with followed me to my own family. It was a cycle that I needed to end.

What did that do for my gem? Well, she learns from me about coping, which she demonstrates now by drinking just like I did, and is always in the same fight-or-flight mode like I used to be.

I remember the day that I decided to baptize her in the Roman Catholic faith which I was forced into by my primary school back in Venezuela. I kept a big reunion, my mom 'cooked up a storm' and everything came out just amazing. But my daughter insisted on hugging me. I was drinking and seeing about my guest, and in the middle of the living room, I pushed her so hard she fell on her butt. I remember that day and still feel a big hole in my stomach. WHY would I do that to my child? And like that instance, I can remember so many others alike.

Meeting my husband was like meeting fresh air. I now see why he became my 'everything'. He, besides God, was the only person to notice how much I used to push away the love of my children. Then he started to correct me. He always said, "Allow yourself to be loved." At first, I could not understand what he meant. Therefore, it took me a while before I allowed my kids to hug me.

Even receiving love from him was something I had to learn to do. After all, no one had ever stopped and shown me how valuable I was; my worth, and said "I love you" just because. And I used to view everything from there. I used to work really hard wherever I was trying to prove to everyone that I was worth it. I had listened to a podcast that said not everything that you learn because of trauma is negative. Because I can see now that my traumas made me an excellent and hardworking person. Anytime I left a job for sure I left a dent, because I used to do my job and everyone else'. Strangely, I do not regret that; I have tons of skills thanks to GOD and I had several good jobs.

Coming back to my girls, I was not the perfect mom, but I did teach my children many good things and I made sure that my children knew their country and culture. I used to take them to the library every Saturday after I got married. We used to go to the Zoo, the cinema, the park, the beach, the countryside, and to the mall. We also visited Venezuela; I took them as far as money allowed me to.

In my own little world, I was doing my best, not realizing the areas where I lacked. And this is what made me forgive my mom. NO parent is a bad parent, and no person is a bad boyfriend or friend. People just copied behaviors that were available to them, because they themselves were victims of that same treatment. We are who we were raised to be.

Yes, just as I was. I see my traumas like being asleep. When you finally wake up and analyze yourself and your behaviors then you realize, *wait, what did I just do? What a mess I did!*

Waking up for me was horrible, I cried for an entire week. Seeing how much I had damaged my kids, my husband, and work relations, and having to let go of people who were downright users and abusers. It was a wake-up call that my life needed. I literally got a second chance; a second life.

*Asking for forgiveness from my sisters and my brothers for my behavior. To my children, I have to explain why I was like that and why I acted like that. That is a responsibility that I had.*

After all, we are humans, something I had to understand. I am grateful for waking up so I can share my experiences to help someone, so that they won't 'Miss the mark'.

Please do not misunderstand me and get offended.

What I mean? We as human beings always get offended when confronted with a truth that resonates with our traumas. I think I can call them triggers.

I will close this chapter by saying that before you go ahead and make plans to build a family, pray about it and check yourself and the way you grew up; your parents, and your emotions. Ask yourself a good question. Am I ok? Because self-righteousness is a real thing. We walk around like we are perfect, and something is wrong with everyone else. Even now that I am emotionally awake, I know that I could be the problem.

Consider this, I had a container with toothpicks, and it turned over. I was able to pick them up and put them back in place. Healing of my traumas was like that. Some people I hurt felt easy to just pick up, but others felt like water that went through a drain. I just had to live with the idea that I did not know better and to forgive myself was the best healthy thing to do. *Forgiveness is more for us.*

***Proverbs 4: 23 KJV***
***Keep thy heart with all diligence; for***
***out of it are the issues of life.***

# 7

# THE LIES I BELIEVED AND LETTING GO

Growing up was tough. I am not going to lie to you and say that it has been a bed of roses. I have cried more than I should. It has been a long, long, long road of ups and downs, and sometimes yes! 'More flour than water' like the old folks would say.

Some mornings I woke up thinking God, I cannot, please show me a way out. But then enlightenment comes, and I realize it is just a phase and GOD IS HERE, ALWAYS!

Learning to let go of my mistakes and all the hurt I had caused and all the lies I believed was a journey that you must take on purpose and with purpose.

No one leading you but the Lord and you making up your mind constantly that you want better because you deserve better, especially if you already have kids and a husband, they deserve the better version of yourself after sticking with you through the worse version of you. And listen, if they did not stick with you, it meant that they were not worthy of this new version, and better is yet to come. Focus on yourself and better yourself.

Growing up I was always angry and bitter.

I was very strict and controlling because of my abandonment trauma. I learned to be there for myself and developed the mentality that everyone was a waste of time. And so, I put up a strong, angered and bitter front. If I wanted something done, I needed to do it myself. I learned that people were a disappointment and that I needed no help. That attitude made me unteachable. I only listened to anyone if I was in 'deep waters' over my head.

This attitude led me to a lot of trouble because my people-pleasing used to get me to far places, but my nonexistent ability used to get me out. As I advanced on my journey, I realized the following truths about my behavior. I used to feel self-sufficient and independent. As some will say I felt I needed no one, but everyone needed me. I used to think that I was more important than everyone, therefore their feelings were not valid to me.

As I worked on myself, I learned these truths about myself:

1. Prayer fixes things
2. People matter to God.
3. People, relationships, and connections are important to get us further in life.

4. No one is an island, and if you try to be you will end up alone and lonely on that island and clearly without supplies.
5. Being independent is important to an extent but at some point, you will need to be interdependent; if you need help, ask for it.
6. Being interdependent will get you to places you have never been.
7. To be a leader you need to submit to leadership.
8. I do not know everything. No one does.
9. Listen to understand, not to respond.
10. The only person I can control is me.
11. You are not responsible for other people's responses, triggers, and the way they behave, therefore, you cannot fix nor control anyone but yourself – your triggers, your responses, and your behavior. Believe me, if you are aware of this, your relationships will flow around you.
12. Watch your thoughts because everything is birthed there.
13. Watch what you are listing to, everything that is all around you feeds you.
14. Watch who influencing you. Your environment is shaping you.
15. Read a good book or listen to nourishing speeches. There are people out there that have conquered the stage where you are at. Not only that, but the Holy Spirit is everywhere to teach you.
16. Read your bible, seeking to understand and put into practice.
17. Do not take anything personally. Because you are feeling offended means that you are being triggered and 100 percent of the time it is not them but, you. Something inside of you is alarming you to check.

Because of how angry I was at God and life for the things I did not have, and for the lack of support in my life, people constantly used to tell me that no one was ever going to marry me. My mom, my sister, my brothers the neighbors; everyone used to repeat over and over that lie to me until it became my own banner. I believed it so much that on the day of my wedding, I awaited something bad to happen. That is why, I believe, the first two years of my marriage were hell. The declaration of the people became my reality. Sadly, I self-sabotaged my own marriage for years.

***Note to self: Refuse Negative Declarations spoken against your life.***

I also used to believe if I laughed too much, something bad would happen. Therefore, I used to be very careful when being happy and try not to be very happy because I felt like something bad will occur and disrupt me. This I believed so much that it really used to come through. Listen, **Proverbs 23:7a records: For as he thinketh in his heart, so is he: ...** Therefore, I could have been manifesting all these good things, but I was outwardly manifesting all kinds of bad things.

I got so upset when I read terms like: "The universe is aligning to give you all that you want in life." People, God is the maker of the universe, and it is the word of God that if you think negatively and listen to negative things and speak negative things you CANNOT live a positive life. It is not the universe giving you or taking away. It is you. The Bible teaches us about the law of sowing and reaping. Whatever your sow you shall reap. You cannot sow tomatoes and expect to reap plantains. You must think positive thoughts, listen to positive messages, and feel positive feelings, and you will live a positive life.

The moment I realized that all this 'stinking thinking' was responsible for my depression and my anger, I started to focus on my thoughts.

I was listening one day to Joyce Meyer Ministries, and she said you can control your thoughts; I was like, *what?* I used to let any thoughts linger in my mind like a playground.

One day I got up thinking that my sister did me wrong and that she was a bad person. I would run around with that thought and it used to grow into a big monster to the point that I could not even speak to her nor look her in the face.

*Thank You, Lord, for deliverance*

Furthermore, I discovered that even what I thought she said was not even about me.

Letting go of that behavior had to take some courage from me to know that people are not placed to get me, they are out trying to survive just as I was. The way I perceived things had to do more with my experiences than with the next person. This I believed for years, that when someone disagreed with me, they were not disapproving of me, they just disapproved of my idea.

It took real courage to look at myself in the mirror and assume responsibility for my thoughts, my actions, and my behavior, and stop running around looking for someone to blame for my disgrace.

I had to stop blaming my circumstances and my trauma for staying like I was. Hurting and telling people off. Yes, I have been hurt. Yes, I was neglected. Yes, I was abused. Yes, I had been abandoned. Yes, no one stopped to help me by the road, but GOD, however, was not an excuse to continue in my illness.

God's mercy was readily available to heal me and to restore me. To rescue me is why Jesus died on the cross. And whosoever the Son of man had set free was free indeed, a new creature in Him.

Facing yourself and your insecurities head-on is the bravest thing you can do for yourself and for those around you. Forgiving yourself for not knowing better, but thanking God for opening your eyes and placing you on solid ground is definitely a plus for your success.

Letting go of the shame, guilt, and the blaming. Understanding what mercy means, and understanding that God did not send His Son to the world to condemn it but to redeem it, is the light on the path to your deliverance.

Know that God wants you to try Him as you have tried everything else, and you know to yourself that nothing worked. Believe me, I have tried everything, drugs, sex, all types of alcohol, men in numbers, friends, even tried quitting, and nothing gave me freedom until I tried Jesus Christ. And thanks to Him, I am a survivor.

I am here sharing my story to tell you that you have hope. As soon as you start listening to the "Word" and stop listening to the world, you will start to feel peace. And brother, sister, yes you will fall a thousand times, but you will get up 1001. Keep going, because the more consistent, disciplined, and perseverant you are with listening to God, the easier it will get. The pits you once easily fell in will allow you to pass, flying.

# 8

# THE END OF IT

I was young and vibrant. I had so much to deal with, and experienced so many moments of discouragements and confusion.

I see young people today going through their different stages of life and I just look back at myself; being a young Christian and a young mother and a young employee and a young friend and young everything. Truth be told, I was a young, 'messed up' individual.

Boy, did I mess up. Yes, I did. But now I am so glad that I could look back and see a few things:

1. Where God took me from
2. The traps the enemy had set to kill me
3. The pain I was in
4. The wrong choices I made
5. The wrong relationship that I kept
6. The anger I channeled in the wrong direction

I sought so much to be understood. Trying to explain to others who I was and what I felt. Today, I stand in my uniqueness. And the reason you are reading this book is proof that you are seeking answers and you are trying to find them here.

The answer is inside of you and always has been, it is just buried under all the pain, the evil, and the wickedness of this world; this world that insists on making you dislike yourself and your uniqueness, all because of experiences.

We each are rare. Stop looking for your identity on social media, where you spend days scrolling, looking for someone like you. There is no one, and you will end up tired and anxious because you are looking for someone to look like.

Start in the mirror, not by looking and listing your so-called imperfections. However, ask yourself WHO TAUGHT you that. Who said you have physical imperfections? Whose validations do you seek? Whose validation really matters? Reintroduce yourself and forget everyone's evil words. They were lying to you.

The truth is that we waste so much time trying for people to like us, and we end up with aborted dreams.

Remind yourself of a few words:

I am unique.
I was perfectly made.
No one is like me.

No one thinks like me.
No one feels like me.
No one looks like me.
No one works like me.
No one sits like me.

AND THAT IS MY SUPERPOWER. And even though it took me long to see, now I know, and I am standing in my UNIQUENESS. Free indeed!

At the end of it all is where I chose to forgive myself for not knowing better and for making the decisions I did at that point in time and honestly, even if no one tells me, they are proud of me. I have gotten to the point where I feel proud of myself for doing what I did with the resources that I had.

You too must find gratefulness, for each one of the stages. Yes, traumas are real, and it is like a force that controls you while you are lying dormant.

We are all built with desires and emotions, and understanding these emotions and why we do certain things is very important. You may not always be pleased by the answer, but the truth is always the best way to go.

Every struggle that I went through had a purpose. I see many characters in the bible, King David, Joseph, Peter, Jeremiah, Daniel, and even Apostle Paul. They really endured very hard trials and according to the scriptures it did not destroy them, but on the opposite, it ended up promoting them. Making them strong, and so I feel.

Not all the symptoms from trauma were negative, I am a resilient woman. I can take a punch. God has used every one of my adversities to mature and strengthen me. And come on, even if I had read this in my twenties, I would still doubt myself saying, *not me, why me, you do not know what you talking about, my pain; my trial is different and you do not understand!*

Yes, I know, but please just give it half of an ear. Every one of life's experiences is here to teach us a lesson that we will need for the future and, get this, the lesson may also be for someone else and you are just the vessel. So, a word of advice my friend is this: do not 'bash' your experiences, rather embrace them, learn from them, seek God for their purpose, and be victorious in achieving it. The only way we learn is by going through.

Let us say for instance, that I have not experienced all those things, how else would I have learnt all the skills I now have? I may not have even been writing this book, and most of all, I would not feel this accomplished today nor be the person I am. Remember when I said, 'I really like me now'? Well, I do.

In life, Jesus, as He told His disciple, will ask you to go to the other side. Dare to go, and do not lose sight that if He asked you to go to the other side, and even if the storm hit your boat, do not doubt that He is with you. So, have faith and be of good courage and learn the lesson that is at hand, because at the end of it, there is freedom.

I think that the greatest freedom is emotional freedom in which you learn to control your emotions and for them not to control you and that you no longer need to prove yourself to anyone, not even to God, because He will never ask you to. He already knows your value and He only wishes that one day you wake up and see you from His eyes. See how wonderful you are.

He showed me how unique I am and it took all my experiences for my uniqueness to surface. I am so glad they did. Whosoever the Son makes free he is free indeed.

As I drafted this book, in every chapter I was seeking your acceptance and your approval, but as I end it I just pray that your heart has been blessed by each one of my testimonies I told you; that once I thought they were going to kill me, but they did not. I am here, a living proof that life gets hard, but you get stronger.

Learn to control your thoughts, your emotions, your reactions, your tongue, and your feelings. And stop, really, please stop meditating on who approves of you. Please do not stop being you. Love yourself. God loves you just the way you are.

Find LIBERTY.

# 9

# LESSON WELL LEARNT

**N**o longer a Victim Lifestyle, Grace had welcomed me

"For Whoever desires to love life and see good days, let him keep his tongue from evil and his lips from speaking deceit; let him turn away from evil and do good; let him seek peace and pursue it."

"For the eyes of the Lord are on the righteous, and his ears are open to their prayer. But the face of the Lord is against those who do evil."

**1 Peter 3:10-12 ESV**

"**I waited patiently for the LORD;** *and he inclined unto me, and heard my cry. 2 He brought me up also out of an horrible pit, out of the miry clay, and set my feet upon a rock, and established my goings.*

**Psalm 40: 1, 2 KJV.**

www.ingramcontent.com/pod-product-compliance
Lightning Source LLC
LaVergne TN
LVHW041551070526
838199LV00046B/1907